Salad Time

2

Salad Time 2

250 MORE Original and Unique Salad Recipes

by Rivky Katz

THE JUDAICA PRESS, INC.

Salad Time 2
© 2007 The Judaica Press, Inc.

Third Printing — June 2012

Other books by this author: *Salad Time & Dessert Time*

ISBN: 978-1-932443-76-9

Proofreader: Hadassa Goldsmith
Cover design and layout: Justine Elliott

THE JUDAICA PRESS, INC.
123 Ditmas Avenue / Brooklyn, NY 11218
718-972-6200 / 800-972-6201
info@judaicapress.com
www.judaicapress.com

Manufactured in the United States of America

The original **Salad Time** quickly rose to popularity among kosher cookbooks. Purely by word-of-mouth, it has sold out of several printings in the few years it's been out.

It's obvious why. Healthy eating is on the rise, and people are looking for fresh and original ideas to incorporate proper nutrition into their diets in an enjoyable way.

Salad Time 2 provides another 250 healthful and delicious salads to satisfy every palate. These recipes are presented with clear instructions and grouped into categories that are as tempting as they are healthy: vegetable salads, fruit salads, pasta salads, dairy salads, meat salads, and dips and dressings. As a bonus, you'll find clever tips and techniques for making salads taste better and last longer.

If you're a salad lover looking to try something different, this book offers a seemingly endless amount of original ideas. Even if salads have never been your thing, you're bound to find recipes in this book that you've never before considered, and that you (or your spouse or children) are sure to enjoy. Hearty appetite!

Rivky Katz

Contents

Salad Tips

- Be organized — prepare all the ingredients you'll need before you begin.

- **Always use fresh vegetables, unless otherwise indicated.**

- When a recipe calls for mangos or avocados, try to buy them a few days in advance and leave them on the counter.

- **Put onions in the refrigerator before cutting them, to keep your eyes from tearing.**

- When a salad recipe calls for meat or poultry, marinate it in the refrigerator overnight before cooking it.

- **When curling vegetables, put them in ice water for 30 minutes so they will hold the curl well.**

- If a salad was placed in the refrigerator, remove it 30 minutes before serving, unless the recipe says to serve it chilled.

- **Attractive presentation makes any salad more appealing.**

- Use lemon slices and purple oriental kale to decorate any fish dish.

- **Always keep the dressing on the side, and pour it on the salad just before serving.**

- Use enough dressing to coat the salad, but not enough to make it soggy.

- **Sprinkle croutons on salads last, so they'll stay crunchy.**

Vegetable
Salads

Artichoke Salad

1 can artichoke hearts
¼ c. sliced onion
1 T. chopped green pepper
1 T. chopped pimento
¼ c. wine vinegar
1 T. oil
1 garlic clove, minced
1 tsp. sugar
Dash black pepper
Dash paprika

Cut artichokes in half. Marinate with rest of ingredients.

Avocado Chili Salad

1 avocado
1 tomato, chopped
1 small onion, chopped
1 tsp. lemon juice
2 tsp. chili powder
1 tsp. salt
Black pepper to taste

Combine all ingredients.

Avocado Guacamole

2 avocados
2 plum tomatoes, chopped
1 small onion, diced
Juice of 1 lime
1 tsp. salt
3 T. chopped cilantro
1 tsp. garlic powder
Dash cayenne pepper

Mash avocados well, add seasonings, then mix in tomatoes and onion.

Avocado & Terra Stix Salad

1 bag romaine lettuce
1 c. spinach leaves
½ c. diced red pepper
½ c. diced yellow pepper
1 avocado
4 oz. pine nuts
6 oz. Terra stix
6 oz. slivered almonds

 Dressing:
⅓ c. oil
⅓ c. red wine vinegar
3 T. ketchup
2 T. grated onion

Place lettuce, spinach and peppers in bowl. Cube avocado and add to vegetables. Add dressing right before serving. Sprinkle pine nuts and Terra stix on top of salad.

Avocado & Tomato Salad

2 ripe avocados
2 ripe tomatoes, diced
½ onion, chopped
2 garlic cloves, minced
2 tsp. Lemon juice
1 tsp. salt
Chili powder to taste

Combine all ingredients.

Avocado with Egg Salad

1 avocado
1 hard-boiled egg, chopped
3 scallions, chopped
1 ½ T. lemon juice
Salt & black pepper

Mix all ingredients together.

Easy Avocado Salad

2 avocados
¼ c. olive oil
Juice of 1 lemon
Salt, garlic powder & black pepper to taste

Blend all ingredients.

Lettuce & Avocado Salad

1 bag romaine lettuce
1 avocado, thinly sliced

 Dressing:
2 T. olive oil
2 tsp. lemon juice
½ tsp. Dijon mustard

Add dressing to lettuce. Place avocado slices on top right before serving.

Marinated Avocado Mix

2 avocados, cut into small pieces
1 package fresh mushrooms, sliced
1 bag purple cabbage
1 purple onion, sliced
1 c. broccoli florets
1 bottle Italian dressing

Place all ingredients in bowl. Let sit for 1 hour before serving.

Spicy Avocado

2 avocados
2 scallions, chopped
1 red pepper, diced
1 green pepper, diced
1 fresh jalapeño pepper, chopped
1/3 c. chopped cilantro
Juice of 1 lemon
Salt to taste

Mash avocado, and add rest of ingredients.

Teriyaki Avocado-Spinach Salad

1 bag baby spinach
1/2 box fresh mushrooms, sliced
1 avocado, sliced
1/2 container grape tomatoes
Bac-O bits
Onion garlic croutons

Dressing:
1/2 c. vinegar
1/2 c. sugar
2 garlic cloves, minced
1/2 c. ketchup
1/2 T. salt
1/2 tsp. mustard
1/2 tsp. teriyaki sauce
3/4 c. oil
1 tsp. paprika

Combine vegetables in bowl. Add dressing. Mix well. Pour Baco bits and croutons over salad.

Vegetable Avocado Salad

1 bag romaine lettuce
1 cucumber, sliced
2 tomatoes, diced
1 avocado, diced

Dressing:
3 T. olive oil
2 T. lime juice
1 T. chopped cilantro
Salt & black pepper

Combine lettuce, tomatoes and cucumber in bowl.
Add dressing. Mix well and add avocado.

Arugula Salad

1 bag arugula salad
1 bag romaine lettuce salad

Dressing:
1 T. balsamic vinegar
Salt & black pepper
1 garlic clove, minced
3 T. olive oil

Mix lettuce leaves with dressing.

Bean Salad

1 c. chickpeas
1 c. cubed Kirbys
2 c. cubed tomatoes
1 c. diced onions
2 T. red wine vinegar
2 T. finely chopped basil
1 T. olive oil
1 T. finely chopped parsley
Salt & black pepper

Mix all ingredients together.

Bean Can Medley Salad

1 can chickpeas
1 can green beans
1 can wax beans
1 green pepper, chopped
1 can corn
1 onion, chopped

Dressing:
½ c. oil
½ c. lemon juice
1 T. oregano
1 T. fresh minced garlic
Salt & black pepper

Mix all vegetables together. Combine with dressing. Mix well.

Bean & Corn Salad

1 box frozen French green beans, defrosted
1 box frozen peas, defrosted
2 11-oz. cans white shoepeg corn, drained
1 green pepper, diced
1 red pepper, diced
1 purple onion, diced
¼ c. oil
2/3 c. vinegar
¼ c. sugar

Mix all ingredients. Marinate for 24 hours

Black Bean Salad

1 15-oz. can black beans, drained & rinsed
½ avocado, diced
2 T. chopped scallions
½ c. chopped tomato
1 T. lime juice
1 T. chopped parsley
1 T. chopped cilantro
Salt & black pepper to taste

Combine lime juice, parsley, cilantro, salt and pepper and stir well.
Add beans, then rest of vegetables, and mix well.

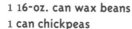

Vegetable Salads

Three Bean Salad

1 16-oz. can string beans
1 16-oz. can wax beans
1 can chickpeas
1 can kidney beans, drained and rinsed
1 can corn
1 medium onion, sliced & separated into rings
1 red pepper, chopped
1 medium onion, sliced & separated into rings
1 garlic clove, chopped

Dressing:
1 c. vinegar
½ c. oil
⅓ c. sugar

Drain all cans. Combine salad ingredients with dressing. Marinate overnight.

Baked Beet Salad

6 large beets

Dressing:
Salt & black pepper
¼ c. white wine vinegar
½ olive oil
1 tsp. cumin
2 green onions, thinly sliced

Wrap each beet tightly in aluminum foil. Place all beets on foil-lined baking sheet. Bake 1 ¼ hours.

Leave on baking sheet; open one corner of each package to let out steam.

After ten minutes, open foil and let stand ten more minutes so skin will peel off easily. Pour dressing over beets, cover with plastic wrap and marinate in refrigerator.

Beet Salad

6 medium-sized beets, tops and roots removed
½ tsp. oregano
2 T. red wine vinegar
1 garlic clove, chopped
2 T. olive oil

Place beets in pot and cover with cold water. Bring to a boil and cook until beets are tender, about 20 minutes. Drain and set aside to cool slightly. Peel beets while still warm, and cut into thick slices. Toss with rest of ingredients.

Beet & Onion Salad

8 medium beets
1 onion, diced
½ c. oil
Squirt lemon juice
1 tsp. fresh garlic
Salt and black pepper

Boil beets in skin until soft. Cut beets in slices. Add rest of ingredients. Mix well.

Warm Beet Salad

6 medium beets
3 T. olive oil
2 T. red wine vinegar
2 garlic cloves, crushed
Salt

Wash beets and boil until tender, about 45 minutes. Remove skin by running cold water over the beets, and then slipping off skins. Slice beets and toss with olive oil, vinegar, garlic and salt.

Vegetable Salads

Bok Choy Salad

1 red pepper, chopped
1 head Bok Choy, chopped
6 scallions, chopped
¼ c. toasted sesame seeds
1 c. thin chow mein noodles
¼ c. toasted sliced almonds

Dressing:
2 T. soya sauce
½ c. Splenda
¼ c. red wine vinegar
¼–½ c. oil

Combine salad ingredients and stir in dressing ingredients
right before serving.

Broccoli Salad

1 bunch fresh broccoli florets
1 c. sliced green olives
1 purple onion, chopped

Dressing:
1 T. sugar
½ c. mayonnaise
2 garlic cloves, crushed

Mix dressing well. Pour over broccoli, olives and onion.

Broccoli & Cashew Salad

1 bag broccoli florets
1 small purple onion, thinly sliced

Dressing:
¾ c. mayonnaise
3 T. sugar
2 T. cider vinegar
4 oz. salted cashews

Mix broccoli and onions with dressing.

Cooked Broccoli Salad

1 bag Bodek broccoli
1 purple onion, sliced & separated into rings

Dressing:
¼ c. red wine vinegar
¾ c. oil
1 tsp. salt
1 garlic clove, crushed
Pinch black pepper

Cook broccoli according to directions on package. Drain. Rinse with cold water. Toss with dressing. Marinate for a few hours.

Sweet Broccoli Salad 1

1 bag broccoli
¼ c. chopped purple onion
½ c. raisins

Dressing:
3 T. vinegar
2 T. sugar
1 c. mayonnaise
1 c. sunflower seeds

Combine broccoli, onions and raisins with dressing.

Sweet Broccoli Salad 2

1 lb. broccoli florets
½ c. craisins
1 purple onion, sliced & separated into rings
Toasted slivered almonds

Dressing:
1 T. vinegar
⅔ c. mayonnaise
¼ c. sugar

Mix all ingredients.

Sweet Broccoli Salad 3

2 bags frozen broccoli florets, thawed
1 bunch chopped scallions
1 handful salted sunflower seeds

Dressing:
1 c. mayonnaise
½ c. sugar
1 T. vinegar

Mix dressing ingredients. Pour over salad before serving.

Tasty Broccoli & Cauliflower Salad 1

1 bunch broccoli, cut in bite-size pieces
1 bunch cauliflower, cut in bite-size pieces
½ box cherry tomatoes
1 purple onion, chopped
1 bottle Italian dressing

Mix all ingredients together. Refrigerate for 2 hours before serving.

Tasty Broccoli & Cauliflower Salad 2

1 bag cauliflower, cut in bite-size pieces
1 bag broccoli, cut in bite-size pieces
2 purple onions, sliced

Dressing:
½ c. mayonnaise
⅓ c. oil
⅓ c. vinegar
¼ c. sugar
½ tsp. salt
¼ tsp. black pepper

Mix dressing ingredients. Pour over salad and chill for several hours.

Bruschetta

2 tomatoes, cut up
1 tsp. olive oil
½ tsp. minced garlic
Fresh basil, chopped
Salt & black pepper to taste

Mix everything well. Serve with bread.

Asian Cabbage Salad

1 bag coleslaw mix
¼ c. toasted sesame seeds
½ c. almonds, thinly sliced
½ purple onion, finely diced
Chinese noodles

Dressing:
½ c. oil
6 T. sugar
½ tsp. salt
6 T. vinegar
¼ tsp. black pepper

Mix well and pour over salad. Add Chinese noodles on top right before serving.

Crunchy Cabbage Salad

1 broccoli coleslaw mix
1 3-oz. package ramen noodles
  (reserve packet of seasoning for dressing)
½ c. slivered almonds
½ c. sunflower seeds
½ c. chopped pecans
½ red pepper, diced
½ green pepper, diced

Dressing:
½ c. oil
¼ c. vinegar
½ c. sugar

Crush noodles and toast over low flame. Add almonds, seeds and pecans, until heated. Mix. Combine nut-noodle mixture with diced peppers. Combine dressing ingredients with Ramen seasoning packets, and pour over salad.

Sweet Cabbage Salad

1 bag green cabbage
2 carrots, shredded

Dressing:
½ c. mayonnaise
4 scallions, sliced
2 tsp. sugar
1 tsp. cumin
Salt & black pepper

Mix cabbage and carrots well with dressing.

Caesar Salad **with Dill**

2 bags salad mix
1 box grape tomatoes

Dressing:
1 c. mayonnaise
¼ c. sugar
¼ c. vinegar
1 tsp. salt
¼ tsp. black pepper
½ bunch dill, chopped

Mix dressing ingredients in blender. Pour over salad.

Classic Caesar Salad 1

1 bag romaine lettuce

Dressing:
4 T. mayonnaise
2 ½ tsp. red wine vinegar
2 T. olive oil
1 garlic clove, minced
Salt & black pepper

Mix dressing ingredients well, and pour over lettuce.

Classic Caesar Salad 2

2 bags romaine lettuce
½ purple onion, thinly sliced
½ box grape tomatoes
Croutons

Dressing:
½ c. mayonnaise
1 tsp. Dijon mustard
1 T. soy sauce
1 T. vinegar
½ tsp. salt
Black pepper
1 garlic clove, minced
¾ c. olive oil

Mix dressing ingredients well. Pour over salad. Add croutons on top.

Crunchy Caesar Salad

1 bag romaine lettuce
2 hard-boiled eggs, sliced
1 package garlic flat breads, broken into pieces

Dressing:
1 c. oil
1 T. sugar
2 raw eggs
½ tsp. soy sauce
¼ tsp. vinegar
1 tsp. mustard
1 tsp. salt
½ tsp. black pepper
1 tsp. garlic powder

Combine dressing with salad. Place flat bread pieces on top.

Italian Caesar Salad

1 bag romaine lettuce
1 tomato, sliced
Onion garlic mini-croutons

Dressing:
½ c. mayonnaise
½ c. Italian dressing
2 T. Dijon mustard
2 T. sugar
Salt & black pepper

Combine lettuce and tomato with dressing. Pour onion garlic mini-croutons on top.

Mixed Caesar Salad

1 bag romaine lettuce
1 purple onion, thinly sliced
1 box grape tomatoes
1 box croutons

Dressing:
¼ c. mayonnaise
¼ c. oil
2 T. Dijon mustard
1 tsp. salt
¼ tsp. crushed garlic
Sprinkle of Mrs. Dash & black pepper

Mix dressing ingredients together. Pour over salad right before serving. Place croutons on top.

Quick & Easy Caesar Salad

1 bag romaine lettuce
3 T. mayonnaise
2 garlic cloves, minced
1 drop of vinegar
Mini-croutons

Mix all ingredients together.

Carrot Salad

1 bag shredded carrots
4 Kirby cucumbers, diced
1 bunch scallions, sliced
½ bunch parsley, chopped
1 T. sugar
3 T. vinegar
Salt & black pepper to taste.

Combine all ingredients.

Pickled Carrot Salad 1

5 large carrots, shredded
3 pickles, diced
1 tomato, diced
1 purple onion, diced

Dressing:
5 T. pickle juice
2 tsp. lemon juice
4 T. mayonnaise
½ c. sugar

Mix dressing well. Pour over salad.

Pickled Carrot Salad 2

1 bag shredded carrots
½ c. chopped sour pickles
3 T. mayonnaise
1 tsp. minced garlic
Salt & black pepper

Combine all ingredients.

Cauliflower Marinade

1 bag cauliflower florets
1 red pepper, chopped
1 small purple onion, chopped
1 can olives
1 small jar pimentos

Dressing:
3 T. cider vinegar
2 T. lemon juice
½ c. oil
2 tsp. salt
¼ tsp. black pepper
1 T. sugar

Mix all ingredients in a bowl. Marinate overnight.

Cauliflower Salad

2 bags frozen cauliflower, defrosted
½ purple onion, diced
1 can of pickles in vinegar

Steam cauliflower. Add onion and pickles. Add mayonnaise, salt & black pepper. Mix and serve at room temperature.

Chickpea Salad 1

1 can chickpeas
1 tomato, chopped
2 garlic cloves, minced
1 purple onion, chopped
½ c. parsley, chopped
3 T. olive oil
1 T. lemon juice
Salt & black pepper

Drain chickpeas. Add to rest of ingredients.

Chickpea Salad 2

2 c. chickpeas
1 purple onion, minced
2 stalks of celery, thinly sliced
1 red pepper, diced

Dressing:
⅓ c. olive oil
5 tsp. lemon juice
Salt & black pepper

Place salad in bowl. Refrigerate a few hours. Just before serving, pour over dressing.

Chopped Eggplant Salad

1 small eggplant
2 hard-boiled eggs
1 T. lemon juice
½ tsp. garlic powder
Salt & black pepper to taste
1 T. mayonnaise
Drop of oil

Bake eggplants until skin separates from eggplant. Place eggplant pulp and eggs in bowl. Chop into very small pieces. Add lemon juice, garlic, salt, black pepper and mayonnaise. Mix well. Stir in oil. Mix until smooth.

Classic Coleslaw 1

1 bag green cabbage
2 carrots, shredded
1 purple onion, sliced
1 green pepper, sliced

Dressing:
1 c. mayonnaise
¼ c. sugar
¼ c. vinegar
Black pepper to taste

Mix dressing well. Pour over coleslaw. Mix well and chill.

Classic Coleslaw 2

2 bags Bodek coleslaw

Dressing:
¼ c. vinegar
½ c. sugar
½ a handful of salt
Dash black pepper
½ c. water
½ 30-oz. jar mayonnaise

Mix dressing with coleslaw. Refrigerate.

Classic Coleslaw 3

1 bag Bodek coleslaw

Dressing:
¼ c. oil
¼ c. sugar
¼ c. vinegar
1 tsp. salt
1 c. mayonnaise

Mix coleslaw with dressing.

Classic Coleslaw 4

1 bag Bodek coleslaw

Dressing:
½ c. mayonnaise
2 T. vinegar
2 T. lemon juice
Salt & black pepper to taste

Mix all ingredients together in bowl. Cover and refrigerate before serving.

Coleslaw with Carrots

6 c. shredded cabbage
1 c. shredded carrots
1 c. mayonnaise
3 T. vinegar
4 T. sugar
1 tsp. salt

Place ingredients in bowl, and mix well.

Coleslaw with Dill

1 bag coleslaw
1 bunch fresh dill, chopped
¼ c. mayonnaise
Dash salt & black pepper

Combine ingredients together and chill.

Easy Coleslaw

1 bag coleslaw

 Dressing:
½ c. mayonnaise
2 T. vinegar
1 T. sugar
Salt
½ tsp. celery seed

Mix dressing well with coleslaw.

Garlic Coleslaw

1 bag coleslaw
Chopped fresh cilantro to taste
1 tomato, chopped
1 cucumber, peeled and chopped

 Dressing:
2 T. vinegar
2 - 4 garlic cloves, crushed
6 T. oil
Salt & black pepper to taste

Mix dressing; let stand for a few hours before pouring over vegetables.

Corn Salad **1**

3 c. corn niblets
1 cucumber, diced
2 sour pickles, diced
1 red pepper, diced
1 onion, diced

Dressing:
3 T. olive oil
½ tsp. mustard
2 T. lemon juice
1 tsp. salt
¼ tsp. black pepper

Combine all ingredients.

Corn Salad **2**

2 cans corn, drained
1 box frozen string beans, defrosted
1 purple onion, chopped
1 red pepper, chopped
1 green pepper, chopped

Dressing:
3 T. sugar
3 T. oil
3 T. vinegar

Combine vegetables with dressing

Corn Salad **3**

1 can corn, drained
1 sour pickle
1 small purple onion, chopped

Dressing:
1 heaping T. mayonnaise
Less than ¼ c. sugar
1 capful vinegar
Salt, black pepper, onion powder
  & garlic powder to taste

Mix all ingredients well.

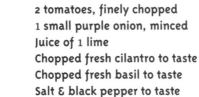

Corn Salad 4

2 cans corn, drained
2 tomatoes, finely chopped
1 small purple onion, minced
Juice of 1 lime
Chopped fresh cilantro to taste
Chopped fresh basil to taste
Salt & black pepper to taste

Mix all ingredients well.

Corn Salad **with Dill**

2 cans corn, drained
4 sour pickles, chopped
2 - 4 T. mayonnaise
Handful of chopped dill
Salt & black pepper to taste

Mix all ingredients well.

Tri-Pepper Corn Salad

2 sour pickles, diced
2 cans corn
½ yellow pepper, diced
½ red pepper, diced
½ orange pepper, diced
½ c. mayonnaise
3 T. vinegar
¼ c. sugar

Drain corn; add rest of ingredients.

White Corn Salad

2 small cans shoepeg (white) corn, drained
1 small can peas, drained
1 purple onion, diced
1 red pepper, diced
1 yellow pepper, diced

Dressing:
¾ c. oil
1 c. water
½ c. sugar
⅓ c. vinegar
1 tsp. salt
1 ½ tsp. black pepper

Mix dressing; pour over salad.

Classic Cucumber Salad 1

4 cucumbers, sliced
1 onion, sliced
½ tsp. salt
½ c. sugar
½ c. lemon juice
½ c. water

Combine all ingredients. Marinate overnight.

Classic Cucumber Salad 2

8 Kirbys, sliced
1 onion, sliced into rings

Dressing:
½ c. sugar
½ c. water
¼ c. vinegar
Handful of dill

Place Kirbys and onions in bowl; salt for ½ hour. Squeeze out or drain excess liquid. Add dressing to vegetables.

Cucumber & Pepper Salad

6 cucumbers, sliced
2 onions, sliced
2 red peppers, sliced

 Dressing:
2 c. vinegar
8 c. water
2 bay leaves
2 c. sugar

Place cucumbers in salted water for 20 minutes. Squeeze out liquid from cucumbers. Combine them with onions and pepper. Mix dressing ingredients, boil and let cool. Add dressing to vegetables. Chill for a few hours.

Cucumber & Radish Salad

8 radishes, sliced
½ c. sliced onion
2 cucumbers, sliced

 Dressing:
2 tsp. oil
1 tsp. sesame oil
Dash salt and crushed red pepper
¼ c. rice wine vinegar

Place radishes, onion and cucumbers in bowl. Pour dressing over salad. Chill before serving.

Dijon Potato Salad

7 red potatoes
2 scallions, chopped
½ c. parsley

 Dressing:
¼ - ½ c. oil
2 T. vinegar
2 tsp. Dijon mustard
½ tsp. salt
Black pepper to taste

Boil potatoes, cut into cubes. Add scallions and parsley. Pour dressing over the vegetables and let sit for 1 hour before serving.

Dijonnaise Salad

1 **bag salad mix**
1 **tomato**
1 **pepper**
1 **cucumber**

Dressing:
¼ **c. mayonnaise**
2 **T. Dijonnaise**
¼ **c. oil**
1 **tsp. salt**
¼ **tsp. crushed garlic**
Black pepper

Mix dressing ingredients and pour over salad.

Eggplant Salad

2 **medium eggplants, peeled & cubed**
8 **peppers: orange, red, yellow and green**
2 **bunches of scallions, chopped**
¾ **c. vinegar**
¼ **c. sugar**
¼ **c. salt**

Place eggplant pieces in 9" x 13" pan and bake, covered,
at 350 degrees for 20 minutes. Boil peppers in pot of water
for 5 minutes. Cut cooked peppers and add them to cooked
eggplant. Add chopped scallions, vinegar, sugar and salt.
Marinate in refrigerator for at least 24 hours, covered.

Gazpacho

1 onion
1 kirby
1 small green pepper
2 garlic cloves
1 T. red wine vinegar
3 T. lemon juice
2 T. soy sauce
2 tsp. hot chopped peppers
1 tsp. salt
Pinch black pepper
1 28-oz. can crushed tomatoes

Combine all ingredients except for crushed tomatoes in food processor. Process until well blended. Add crushed tomatoes. Refrigerate.

Green Salad

1 bag lettuce
1 bag shredded green cabbage
2 c. chopped tomatoes
2 cucumbers, sliced
1 c. shredded carrots

 Dressing:
2 T. olive oil
2 T. fresh chopped cilantro
2 garlic cloves, minced
1 tsp. salt

Mix all ingredients.

Green Cabbage Salad

1 bag shredded green cabbage
1 T. olive oil
1 T. chopped scallions
2 T. chopped parsley
2 T. lemon juice
Salt & black pepper

Combine all ingredients. Mix well.

Green & Red Salad

4 tomatoes
2 cucumbers
1 small onion
½ c. green pepper
¼ c. green olives, sliced
1 tsp. chopped parsley

Dressing:
1 garlic clove, minced
½ tsp. salt
¼ tsp. black pepper
¼ c. lemon juice
¼ c. oil

Mix dressing ingredients. Chop vegetables and pour dressing over them. Chill for 2 hours before serving.

Green & Red Cabbage Salad

1 bag shredded green cabbage
1 bag shredded red cabbage
2 carrots, shredded
1 onion, chopped
½ c. raisins (optional)

Dressing:
⅓ c. olive oil
2 T. orange juice
5 T. cider vinegar
2 tsp. sugar
Salt & black pepper to taste

Whisk dressing until thickened. Pour dressing over vegetables. Marinate overnight.

Crunchy Health Salad

4 cucumbers, cubed
1 green pepper, sliced long & thin
1 red pepper, diced
1 small purple onion, sliced
2 carrots, sliced round
1 can baby corn, drained & cut in half

 Dressing:
½ c. oil
½ c. vinegar
¾ c. sugar
4 T. water
Less than 3 tsp. salt

Mix dressing, pour over salad and marinate overnight.

Health Salad

4 cucumbers, sliced
1 red pepper, sliced
1 green pepper, sliced
1 purple onion, diced
4 carrots, sliced

 Dressing:
½ c. vinegar
4 tsp. water
¾ c. sugar
3 tsp. salt
¼ c. oil

Place all vegetables in bowl. Pour dressing over salad. Marinate overnight.

Health Salad Slaw

1 bag coleslaw mix
1 cucumber, sliced
1 pepper, diced
1 tomato, cut into chunks
1 medium onion, chopped

Dressing:
½ c. wine vinegar
½ c. water
½ c. sugar
2 tsp. salt
Garlic powder & black pepper to taste

Place vegetables in bowl. Pour dressing over salad.
Marinate overnight.

Hearts of Palm Salad 1

1 can hearts of palm, drained & sliced
1 avocado, diced
½ box cherry tomatoes, sliced
½ c. chopped dill weed

Dressing:
4 T. oil
4 T. vinegar
Dash black pepper
Dash salt

Mix dressing; pour over salad. Sprinkle chopped dill weed over
top of salad.

Hearts of Palm Salad 2

1 can hearts of palm, drained & sliced
½ c. chopped purple onion
1 c. halved cherry tomatoes
2 avocados, diced
1 T. mayonnaise
Juice of ½ lemon
Salt & black pepper to taste.

Mix all ingredients well.

Hearts of Palm
Can Medley Salad

1 can hearts of palm,
1 can baby corn
1 can olives, sliced
1 can chickpeas
1 tomato, sliced
1 cucumber, sliced
1 bottle fat free dressing

Drain all cans. Pour dressing over salad and mix well.

Fancy Hearts of Palm Salad

1 can hearts of palm, drained and sliced
1 can baby corn, cut into pieces
1 box grape tomatoes, cut in half
¼ lb. fresh snow peas, cut in half
1 can chickpeas, drained

 Dressing:
¼ olive oil
⅓ c. vinegar
4 tsp. sugar
2 cloves fresh garlic, minced
¼ tsp. oregano
¼ tsp. basil
1 tsp. salt
¼ tsp. dry mustard
1 tsp. dill

Mix dressing well; pour over salad.

Italian Hearts of Palm Salad

1 can hearts of palm, drained & sliced
½ box grape tomatoes, halved
1 cucumber, diced
1 can chickpeas, drained
1 can baby corn, drained & cut in half
1 bottle Italian dressing

Combine all ingredients in a large bowl.

Hummus with Tahini

1 15-oz. can of chickpeas, drained
1 c. tahini paste
1 fresh lemon
2 garlic cloves, crushed
Cumin, salt & paprika to taste
Olive oil
Parsley for garnish

Purée chickpeas, tahini paste, 1 teaspoon oil, lemon juice and spices in blender. When serving, pour olive oil on top and garnish with parsley.

Hummus

1 15-oz. can chickpeas, drained
1 T. lemon juice
1 T. olive oil
2 garlic cloves, minced
2 T. chopped parsley
2 scallions, sliced
Salt & black pepper to taste

In food processor, place chickpeas, lemon juice, oil and garlic. Add more olive oil slowly until it is the consistency of purée. Place hummus in bowl and add parsley, scallions and seasoning to taste.

Israeli Salad

1 sour pickle
2 cucumbers
4 medium tomatoes
1 small red or yellow pepper, finely diced

Dressing:
2 T. chopped scallions
3 - 4 T. chopped parsley
1 - 2 T. Balsamic vinegar
Salt & black pepper to taste.

Cut vegetables into small pieces. Pour dressing over salad and mix well.

Kale Salad

1 bunch kale leaves, very well cleaned
1 avocado, chopped
¼ purple onion, sliced
½ box cherry tomatoes, halved

 Dressing:
1 fresh lemon
Olive oil as desired
Sprinkle of garlic powder

Place all vegetables in bowl. Squeeze lemon juice on top. Add oil and garlic powder. Mix well.

Lettuce Salad

1 bag romaine lettuce

 Dressing:
Juice of 1 large lemon
3 garlic cloves, minced
½ c. olive oil
salt to taste

Mix dressing ingredients together and pour over salad just before serving.

Lettuce & Almond Salad

1 bag lettuce
½ box grape tomatoes
1 c. caramelized almonds

 Dressing:
3 T. sugar
3 T. vinegar
3 T. olive oil

Mix dressing with lettuce and tomatoes. Sprinkle almonds on top.

Marinated Salad

4 cucumbers, cubed
1 red pepper, diced
1 green pepper, cut into long slices
1 purple onion, sliced into rings
2 carrots, sliced into round pieces
1 can baby corn, drained

Dressing:
½ c. vinegar
½ c. oil
½ - ¾ c. sugar
4 T. water
2 ½ tsp. salt

Mix dressing, pour over salad and marinate overnight.

Marinated Mushroom Salad

1 box fresh mushrooms, sliced
1 bag broccoli florets
1 zucchini, sliced
1 red pepper, sliced
1 can water chestnuts, drained & sliced
1 purple onion, sliced

Dressing:
¾ c. low-fat Italian dressing
¼ c. balsamic vinegar
¼ c. honey

Mix all ingredients well in a bowl, and marinate overnight.

Mixed Salad

1 bag shredded carrots
½ bunch celery, sliced
1 medium purple onion, sliced
1 red pepper, sliced
1 green pepper, sliced
½ box fresh mushrooms, sliced
1 zucchini, sliced

 Dressing:
¾ c. mayonnaise
1 tsp. salt
⅓ c. olive oil
½ c. sugar
½ c. vinegar

Mix all ingredients in bowl. Refrigerate for one day before serving.

Mushroom Salad (warm)

1 bag baby spinach leaves
2 T. olive oil
½ box fresh mushrooms, sliced

 Dressing:
5 T. olive oil
1 T. Balsamic vinegar
1 tsp. Dijon mustard
Sugar, salt & black pepper to taste

Heat oil in pan and add mushrooms for 5 minutes until tender. Pour dressing over mushrooms in pan, heat for a few minutes and then pour mushroom mixture over spinach leaves. Serve immediately.

Mushroom Soy Salad

½ box fresh mushrooms, sliced
1 bag arugula
1 purple onion, chopped

Dressing:
6 T. olive oil
3 T. lemon juice
1 tsp. soy sauce
Salt & black pepper to taste

Mix dressing ingredients and pour over salad just before serving.

Sweet Mushroom Salad

1 bag lettuce
1 can whole mushrooms
1 can hearts of palm
1 can baby corn

Dressing:
¼ c. sugar
¼ c. vinegar
¼ c. oil
Salt & black pepper

Drain all cans. Mix vegetables with lettuce. Combine with dressing.

Pepper Salad

2 red peppers, sliced
1 yellow pepper, sliced
1 orange pepper, sliced
1 box grape tomatoes
1 avocado, cubed
1 can hearts of palm, drained & sliced
Pine nuts

Dressing:
¼ c. olive oil
½ tsp. salt
black pepper
garlic powder
4 T. lemon juice
3 - 4 T. sugar

Mix dressing well and pour over salad.

Potato Salad 1

5 medium potatoes
¼ c. small pieces of sour pickle
2 hard-boiled eggs, chopped
½ c. mayonnaise
1 small onion, finely chopped
¼ c. green olives, sliced
Salt & black pepper to taste
Dash garlic powder

Cook potatoes, drain and cut. Add rest of ingredients and mix well.

Potato Salad 2

2 c. cooked, peeled and cubed potatoes
1 sour pickle, chopped
¼ c. peas
3 T. mayonnaise
2 T. olive oil
Salt & black pepper

Combine all ingredients and toss well. Chill and serve.

Potato Salad 3

6 potatoes
½ onion, chopped
1 pickle, chopped
¼ c. shredded carrots

 Dressing:
3 T. mayonnaise
Dash sugar & lemon juice
Salt & black pepper

Peel and cook potatoes, and cut into cubes. Add potatoes to rest of ingredients.

Red Potato Salad

2 lbs. red potatoes, cooked & quartered

Dressing:
¼ c. diced purple onion
1 c. mayonnaise
¼ c. Dijonnaise
2 T. vinegar
2 T. chopped fresh dill
½ tsp. salt
¼ tsp. black pepper

Combine dressing with potatoes while still hot.

Tangy Potato Salad

5 potatoes, cubed
½ c. finely diced white onion
1 c. mayonnaise
2 T. white vinegar
1 ½ tsp. salt
1 tsp. sugar
Dash white pepper & paprika

Cook potatoes and drain well. Combine potatoes with rest of
ingredients. Sprinkle white pepper & paprika on top and chill.

Portobello Mushroom Salad

3 pkgs. Portobello mushrooms, sliced
2 bags Euro salad
1 box grape tomatoes
Pine nuts
½ box onion garlic croutons

 Dressing:
¼ tsp. dry mustard
¼ c. ketchup
¼ c. vinegar
½ c. olive oil
½ c. sugar
1 garlic clove, crushed
½ tsp. salt
¼ tsp. paprika

Clean, cube and sauté mushrooms until shriveled. Place contents of salad bags and tomatoes in bowl. Place croutons on top. Mix dressing and pour over salad. Place mushrooms on top.

Teriyaki Portobello Mushroom Salad

1 pkg. portobello mushrooms, diced
1 ½ tsp. teriyaki sauce
1 bag mesclun leaves
Cherry tomatoes
Handful candied almonds

 Dressing:
⅔ c. oil
¼ c. sugar
¼ c. balsamic vinegar
¼ c. ketchup
2 garlic cloves, crushed
¼ tsp. dry mustard
¼ tsp. paprika

Sauté mushrooms until soft. Drain. Pour teriyaki sauce over mushrooms and cook over low flame for a few minutes. Place mushrooms over vegetables, and pour dressing over salad. Place almonds on top just before serving.

Radish Salad

4 c. radishes, sliced
½ c. thinly sliced onions
1 c. diced tomatoes
Fresh chopped parsley

Dressing:
1 ¼ tsp. salt
1 small garlic clove, minced
⅛ tsp. black pepper
1 tsp. chopped fresh basil
2 T. lemon juice
2 T. oil

Combine radish, tomato and onion. Whisk together dressing
ingredients, pour over salad and garnish with parsley.

Crunchy Red Cabbage Salad

1 bag shredded red cabbage
1 bag salad mix
1 c. slivered almonds, toasted

Dressing:
⅓ c. oil
⅓ c. vinegar
⅓ c. honey
½ tsp. salt

Mix dressing well and pour over salad.

Red Cabbage Salad

1 bag shredded red cabbage
1 small onion, minced
⅓ c. oil
⅓ c. vinegar
1 T. sugar
Salt & black pepper to taste.

Mix all ingredients well.

Red Cabbage Salad with a Twist

1 bag shredded red cabbage
1 T. olive oil
1 T. vinegar
1 tsp. sugar
2 T. lemon juice
Salt & black pepper

Mix all ingredients well.

Rice Salad

8 c. cooked rice, cooled
½ c. diced green pepper
½ c. minced onion
¼ c. parsley, chopped
¼ c. diced pimento
1 c. black olives, halved
¾ c. oil
¼ c. vinegar
Salt & pepper to taste

Place all ingredients in large bowl. Mix well.

Salad with Flatbreads

1 bag romaine lettuce
1 bag shredded purple cabbage
1 box grape tomatoes
10 oz. garlic flatbreads, broken into pieces

 Dressing:
¾ tsp. salt
1 tsp. black pepper
1 tsp. dry mustard
½ c. mayonnaise
¾ c. olive oil
1 T. tamari soy sauce
2 garlic cloves, minced
1 tsp. lemon juice

Mix dressing, and pour over salad. Sprinkle flatbreads on top.

Spicy Pepper Slaw

3 red peppers, thinly sliced
2 red hot peppers, minced
2/3 c. olive oil
1/2 c. red wine vinegar
1 bag green cabbage
Salt to taste

Toss both peppers in bowl. Boil oil, sugar and vinegar, and pour over peppers. Add cabbage and season with salt.

Spicy Tomatoes

4 tomatoes, sliced
1/3 c. thinly sliced scallions
1/3 c. chopped celery
4 garlic cloves, minced
1 red hot pepper, thinly sliced

Dressing:
1/3 c. balsamic vinegar
1 T. olive oil
1 T. brown sugar
2 tsp. minced fresh ginger
1 tsp. cumin
Salt & black pepper to taste

Blend dressing well, pour over tomato salad and refrigerate.

Asian Crunch Spinach Salad

1 bag spinach leaves
1 purple onion, sliced
1 can water chestnuts, drained
1 red pepper, sliced
6 fresh mushrooms, sliced

Dressing:
1 tsp. soy sauce
1/3 c. lemon juice
1/4 c. olive oil
1/4 c. sugar
1 tsp. salt

Mix dressing well and pour over salad.

Baby Spinach Salad

1 16-oz. bag baby spinach
8 - 10 fresh mushrooms, sliced
1 8-oz. can sliced water chestnuts, drained
4 T. imitation bacon bits
6 oz. fresh snow peas
Chinese noodles

Dressing:
½ c. oil
⅓ c. ketchup
½ purple onion, minced
⅓ c. sugar
¼ c. apple cider vinegar
1 tsp. Worcestershire sauce

Mix dressing and pour over salad. Sprinkle Chinese noodles on top.

Spinach Salad 1

1 bag fresh spinach
1 purple onion, sliced into rings
½ bag purple cabbage
1 box cherry tomatoes, cut into half
1 avocado, diced

Dressing:
1 ¼ c. oil
2 tsp. Dijon mustard
1 small onion, finely chopped
½ c. red wine vinegar
½ c. sugar
½ c. honey
Black pepper to taste

Blend dressing ingredients and pour over salad. Mix well.

Spinach Salad 2

2 10 oz. bags fresh spinach
1 15-oz. can hearts of palm, drained
1 box grape tomatoes
2 avocados, peeled & chopped
8 oz. fresh mushrooms, sliced
½ c. sliced almonds

Dressing:
¼ c. sugar
½ tsp. salt
½ tsp. dry mustard
¼ tsp. paprika
⅜ c. oil
3 T. white vinegar
¼ c. ketchup
1 garlic clove, minced

Mix dressing well and pour over salad.

Spinach & Avocado Salad

1 bag spinach leaves
1 avocado, diced
1 box fresh mushrooms, sliced
1 box cherry tomatoes
garlic croutons

Dressing:
½ c. vinegar
½ c. sugar
2 garlic cloves, crushed
½ c. ketchup
½ T. salt
½ tsp. dry mustard
½ tsp. paprika
1 ½ c. oil

Mix dressing well and pour over salad.

Warm Spinach Salad

1 bag spinach leaves
4 mushrooms, sliced
1 shallot, minced
1 tsp. red wine vinegar
2 T. olive oil
¼ c. walnuts, chopped
Salt & black pepper to taste

Combine shallots, vinegar and salt (to taste) in bowl. Heat oil over medium heat and add walnuts, stirring until lightly browned. Remove walnuts and add to spinach. Place mushrooms in pan and cook for 3 minutes. Remove and add to spinach. Combine with shallot mixture and toss well. Add salt and black pepper to taste.

String Bean Salad

1 lb string beans, ends trimmed
1 garlic clove, chopped
Salt & black pepper to taste
2 T. red wine vinegar
¼ c. olive oil

Bring large pot of salted water to boil, and add string beans. Cook for about 7 minutes. Remove string beans and allow to cool. In a small bowl, mix together garlic, salt, black pepper and vinegar. Gradually whisk in olive oil.

Pour dressing over cooled string beans and toss.

Sweet & Sour Cabbage Salad

1 bag shredded red cabbage
1 bag shredded green cabbage
2 carrots, shredded
¼ c. sunflower seeds
1 c. mini-croutons

Dressing:
½ c. olive oil
¼ c. red wine vinegar
¼ c. lemon juice
1 T. onion soup mix
¼ c. sugar

Place all salad ingredients in large bowl. Mix dressing ingredients and add to salad. Top with croutons.

Tabouleh

1 c. cracked wheat, cooked & drained
2 tomatoes, finely diced
1 bunch scallions, green & white parts, chopped
1 bunch parsley, chopped
¼ c. olive oil
⅓ c. lemon juice
Salt & black pepper to taste

Mix all ingredients well. Refrigerate before serving.

Zesty Tabouleh

1 c. bulgur wheat
2 c. boiling water
4 kirbys, finely diced
2 tomatoes, finely diced
Chopped parsley
½ c. chickpeas

 Dressing:
2 tsp. cumin
2 tsp. chopped mint leaves
1 T. salt
6 T. oil
Juice of 2-3 fresh lemons

Pour boiling water over wheat and let sit, covered, for ½ hour until the water is well absorbed. Drain. Add wheat to vegetables and chickpeas, pour dressing over salad and mix well.

Tahini Salad

1 bag romaine lettuce
2 - 3 tomatoes, finely chopped
2 - 3 cucumbers, finely chopped
1 bunch parsley, chopped
1 bunch scallions, green and white parts, chopped
Salt & black pepper
½ c. olive oil
1 c. tahini
Juice of 2 lemons

In a bowl, combine all ingredients except tahini and lemon juice. In another bowl, mix tahini with a drop of water. Add lemon juice, stir and mix with vegetables.

Basic Tomato Salad

4 - 6 tomatoes, sliced
2 scallions, sliced
¼ c. oil
2 T. water
1 T. sugar
Salt & black pepper to taste
2 - 3 T. lemon juice
Sprinkle of fresh parsley

Mix all ingredients in bowl.

Creamy Tomato & Cucumber Salad

4 tomatoes, sliced
1 cucumber, sliced
½ purple onion, diced
¼ c. mayonnaise
2 garlic cloves, minced
Salt & black pepper

Combine all ingredients.

Crunchy Tomato Salad

2 tomatoes, sliced
1 cucumber, sliced
1 pepper, sliced
1 stalk celery, sliced
3 T. vinegar
1 T. sugar
Salt & black pepper to taste

Combine all ingredients.

Easy Tomato Salad

6 tomatoes, sliced
1 onion, sliced

 Dressing:
3 T. olive oil
1 T. vinegar
1 T. chopped parsley
Salt & black pepper to taste

Combine tomatoes and onion in bowl. Pour dressing over salad. Mix well.

Marinated Tomato Salad

4 tomatoes, sliced
½ c. diced purple onion
½ c. chopped parsley

 Dressing:
½ c. olive oil
½ tsp. oregano
¼ c. red wine vinegar
1 garlic clove, minced
Salt & black pepper

Combine ingredients. Refrigerate before serving.

Solo Tomato Marinade

8 - 10 large tomatoes, sliced

 Dressing:
½ c. olive oil
½ c. red wine vinegar
½ tsp. black pepper
½ tsp. salt
1 tsp. garlic powder
1 tsp. oregano
2 tsp. minced onion

Mix dressing and pour over tomatoes. Marinate overnight.

Sweet Tomato Salad

4 tomatoes, sliced
1 avocado, cubed
1 can hearts of palm, drained & sliced
1 purple onion, sliced

Dressing:
¼ c. olive oil
¼ c. vinegar
6 - 8 tsp. sugar
1 tsp. salt

Mix dressing. Pour over vegetables just before serving.

Tomato & Cucumber Salad

2 tomatoes, sliced
1 cucumber, diced
1 onion, finely diced
1 T. lemon juice
Salt & black pepper

Combine all ingredients.

Tomato & Onion Salad

4 tomatoes, chopped
1 purple onion, diced
1 white onion, diced
¼ c. sliced black olives

Dressing:
1 tsp. vinegar
Squirt of lemon juice
Salt & black pepper to taste

Mix dressing and pour over salad. Serve with flatbreads and feta cheese.

Tomato & Pepper Salad

4 tomatoes, sliced
1 red pepper, cut into strips
1 bunch parsley, chopped

Dressing:
⅓ c. olive oil
Balsamic vinegar
Salt & black pepper to taste

Mix dressing, pour over salad and toss well.

Tomato & Pine Nut Salad

4 tomatoes, chopped
8 - 10 oven-dried tomato halves, sliced
1 c. arugula leaves
4 T. pine nuts
3 T. olive oil
1 T. lemon juice
Salt & black pepper to taste

Place tomatoes and arugula in broiler and broil for a few minutes. Toast pine nuts and add to tomatoes. Pour oil and lemon juice over salad. Season with spices.

Tomato Basil Salsa

2 c. tomatoes, seeded, peeled and chopped
¼ c. chopped fresh basil
2 T. chopped purple onion
2 T. red wine vinegar
Salt & black pepper to taste

Combine all ingredients in bowl.

Tomato Chive Salad

12 plum tomatoes, sliced
1 purple onion, sliced
3 T. chives
½ c. oil
½ c. vinegar
½ c. sugar
1 tsp. garlic powder
1 tsp. salt
1 tsp. black pepper

Combine all ingredients in bowl. Marinate for a few hours.

Tomato Corn Salsa

1 box cherry tomatoes, chopped
1 tsp. salt
1 can corn, drained
2 T. lemon juice
2 T. chopped cilantro
1 garlic clove, minced
3 tsp. olive oil
Salt & black pepper to taste

Combine tomatoes and salt well. Combine with rest of
ingredients and toss well.

Tomato Cumin Salad

2 tomatoes, diced
½ c. diced onion
¼ c. chopped parsley
1 garlic clove, minced
½ tsp. salt
Cumin & black pepper to taste

Mix all ingredients together. Refrigerate for 1 hour.

Tomato Herb Salad

5 tomatoes, sliced
1 onion, sliced
1 cucumber, sliced
1 green pepper, chopped
½ c. fresh basil, chopped
½ c. fresh parsley, chopped
2 T. crushed garlic
2 T. vinegar
Salt & black pepper to taste

Combine all ingredients.

Tomato Mushroom Salad

2 boxes cherry tomatoes
1 lb. fresh mushrooms
1 purple onion

 Dressing:
⅓ c. apple cider vinegar
⅓ c. water
⅓ c. oil
1 tsp. salt
¼ tsp. garlic powder
⅛ tsp. black pepper
Basil & oregano to taste

Slice cherry tomatoes and mushrooms into quarters. Slice onion. Combine dressing ingredients and pour over vegetables. Cover and marinate for at least a few hours.

Tomato Olive Marinade

4 tomatoes, sliced
½ c. olives, sliced
1 medium onion, sliced into rings

 Dressing:
1 T. vinegar
¼ c. oil
¼ tsp. salt

Combine tomatoes, olives and onion. Add vinegar, oil and salt. Marinate overnight.

Tomato Olive Salad 1

4 tomatoes, sliced
1 purple onion, sliced
¼ c. chopped parsley
2 T. chopped green olives
2 T. red wine vinegar
1 T. olive oil
Salt & black pepper to taste

In large bowl, place all ingredients except vinegar and oil.
Mix vinegar and oil well in blender. Add to salad just before
serving.

Tomato Olive Salad 2

3 tomatoes, sliced
1 c. sliced green or black olives
¼ c. olive oil
2 T. oregano
2 garlic cloves, minced
1 T. balsamic vinegar
1 tsp. salt

Mix all ingredients together in bowl.

Tomato Parsley Salad

4 medium tomatoes
6 T. chopped fresh parsley
1 garlic clove
6 T. olive oil
2 T. white vinegar
1 tsp. salt
1 T. chopped basil
black pepper to taste
1 bunch scallions, finely chopped

Put tomatoes and parsley in bowl. Mix remaining ingredients
except scallions in blender and pour over tomatoes. Place
scallions on top.

Tri-Color Salad

1 box frozen cauliflower florets, thawed
1 box frozen broccoli florets, thawed
1 red pepper, chopped
1 green pepper, chopped
1 purple onion, chopped

Dressing:
1 c. mayonnaise
½ c. oil
⅓ c. vinegar
½ c. sugar

Mix dressing ingredients. Mix with salad. Marinate at least 2 hours before serving.

Tuna Salad

1 can tuna
1 can water chestnuts, drained & chopped
½ small onion, chopped
1 stalk celery, chopped
½ c. shredded carrots
½ c. mayonnaise
1 T. Dijon mustard
1 tsp. soy sauce
Salt & black pepper
Lettuce

Mix ingredients together. Place on bed of lettuce and chill.

Salads with Fruit

Autumn Green Salad

1 bag romaine lettuce
1 purple onion, sliced
½ c. toasted pine nuts
1 green apple, sliced
1 c. craisins

 Dressing:
½ c. canola oil
¼ c. rice vinegar
3 T. sugar
1 T. poppy seeds
1 tsp. dry mustard powder
1 tsp. salt

Mix dressing. Place vegetables and fruit in a bowl. Pour dressing over the salad and mix well.

Avocado Salad

1 bag romaine lettuce
½ avocado, sliced
1 red pepper, sliced
1 purple onion, sliced
1 can mandarin oranges
slivered almonds

 Dressing:
1 c. oil
½ small onion
1 tsp. dry mustard powder
½ c. vinegar
½ c. sugar

Blend dressing well and pour over the salad right before serving.

Broccoli Orange Salad

1 bunch broccoli
½ c. raisins
½ c. chopped purple onion
1 small can mandarin oranges, drained
1 8-oz. can water chestnuts, drained
1 c. sunflower seeds

 Dressing:
1 c. mayonnaise
⅓ c. sugar
2 T. vinegar

Mix salad ingredients and pour dressing over it. Add sunflower
seeds just before serving.

Broccoli Raisin Salad

1 bag broccoli
½ c. raisins
½ c. sunflower seeds
¼ c. chopped purple onion
1 c. frozen peas, thawed

 Dressing:
1 c. mayonnaise
2 T. vinegar
½ c. sugar

Mix dressing ingredients together. Pour over salad just
before serving.

Carrot Salad

6 medium carrots, grated
2 large apples, grated
4 T. sugar
2 T. lemon juice
1 c. orange juice

Mix all ingredients together and refrigerate.

Euro Salad

1 bag Euro salad mix
1 box strawberries
2 mangos, cut into pieces
2 handfuls craisins
2 handfuls candied pecans

Dressing:
½ c. oil
½ c. sugar
¼ c. vinegar
1 tsp. salt

Boil dressing and pour over salad.

European Salad

1 bag romaine lettuce
1 mango, cubed
1 box fresh strawberries, sliced
¾ c. cranberries
1 lb. honey glazed almonds

Dressing:
¼ c. vinegar
½ c. sugar
½ c. oil
1 tsp. salt

Combine salad ingredients. Cook dressing ingredients over low heat for 5 minutes, stirring constantly. Let dressing cool. Pour dressing over salad immediately before serving.

Macadamia Nut Salad

2 c. alfalfa sprouts
2 c. shredded carrots
2 stalks celery, sliced
½ pkg. shredded red cabbage
1 c. raisins
Macadamia nuts

Dressing:
½ c. mayonnaise
1 tsp. salt
¼ c. sugar
black pepper

Place vegetables in bowl. Pour dressing over salad. Place macadamia nuts on top.

Crunchy Mandarin Orange Salad

1 bag lettuce
1 bag shredded red cabbage
4 cucumbers, sliced
2 cans mandarin oranges, drained
1 bag thin chow mein noodles
½ c. roasted sunflower seeds
½ c. slivered almonds

Dressing:
½ c. oil
4 T. brown sugar
6 T. vinegar
1 tsp. salt

Combine salad with dressing. Place chow mein noodles on top of salad.

Salads with Fruit

Mandarin Salad

1 bag Euro salad
1 bag shredded red cabbage
1 can mandarin oranges, drained
Handful craisins
Handful slivered almonds, toasted

Dressing:
4 T. brown sugar
½ c. oil
6 T. vinegar
1 tsp. salt

Mix dressing and pour over salad.

Mandarin Craisin Salad

1 can mandarin oranges, drained
1 c. craisins
1 bag lettuce

Dressing:
4 T. balsamic vinegar
4 T. sugar
½ c. olive oil
Salt & black pepper to taste

Mix dressing and pour over salad.

Mango Salsa

2 c. diced mango
½ c. chopped red pepper
½ c. chopped purple onion
2 T. fresh lemon juice
4 T. chopped cilantro
1 tsp. grated lemon rind

Mix all ingredients.

Mango Salad

4 mangos, cubed
1 box strawberries, sliced
1 bag lettuce
½ bag toasted almonds
¾ container craisins
1 purple onion, chopped

Dressing:
½ c. oil
½ c. vinegar
½ c. sugar
Pinch of salt

Mix dressing and pour over salad. Mix well.

Orange & Spinach Salad

1 bag baby spinach leaves
2 oranges, sliced
½ purple onion

Dressing:
3 T. olive oil
2 T. freshly squeezed orange juice
2 tsp. lemon juice
1 tsp. honey
½ tsp. mustard
Salt & black pepper

Mix dressing well. Pour over salad just before serving.

Oriental Salad

1 head lettuce
3 scallions, sliced
1 can mandarin oranges, drained
1 c. Chinese noodles
1 c. slivered almonds
¼ c. sunflower seeds

 Dressing:
6 T. tarragon vinegar
4 T. brown sugar
½ c. oil
1 tsp. salt

Mix dressing and pour over salad.

Poppy Seed Salad

1 bag romaine lettuce
1 purple onion, sliced
1 c. craisins

 Dressing:
½ c. mayonnaise
⅓ c. sugar
¼ c. non-dairy milk
2 T. vinegar
1 T. poppy seeds

Mix dressing well. Toss with salad just before serving.

Rice Salad

2 c. cooked rice
1 c. pine nuts
1 c. sliced mushrooms
½ c. bean sprouts
½ c. golden raisins
1 shallot
1 T. parsley flakes
½ c. thin chow mein noodles

 Dressing:
½ c. oil
¼ c. soy sauce
2 garlic cloves, crushed

Cook rice and add salad ingredients. Pour dressing over salad and top with chow mein noodles.

Baby Spinach Salad

2 bags baby spinach
sliced fresh mushrooms
shredded carrots
1 avocado, cubed
Handful blueberries
1 purple onion, sliced

 Dressing:
½ jar raspberry vinaigrette dressing
¼ c. mayonnaise
¼ tsp. sugar
2 T. vinegar
dash salt and garlic powder

Mix dressing well and pour over salad.

Spinach & Orange Salad

1 bag spinach leaves
2 oranges, sliced

Dressing:
¼ c. honey
¼ c. balsamic vinegar
2 T. olive oil
1 tsp. Dijon mustard
Salt & black pepper

Mix dressing. Place spinach and oranges in bowl. Drizzle dressing over salad just before serving.

Spinach & Strawberry Salad

1 bag spinach leaves
1 pint strawberries, sliced
Slivered almonds, toasted
Fresh mushrooms, sliced

Dressing:
¾ c. oil
½ tsp. salt
½ c. apple cider vinegar
1 T. Dijon mustard
¼ c. sugar
3 T. minced purple onion

Blend dressing until smooth. Pour over rest of ingredients.

Strawberry Poppy Seed Salad

1 bag lettuce
1 purple onion, diced
1 c. sliced strawberries

Dressing:
1 c. mayonnaise
²⁄₃ c. sugar
¼ c. vinegar
½ c. water
2 T. poppy seeds

Mix dressing and pour over salad just before serving.

String Bean Salad

2 lbs string beans
2 c. dried mango, chopped
4 scallions, chopped
¼ c. unsalted sunflower seeds
½ c. chopped pecans

 Dressing:
2 small garlic cloves, minced
2 T. honey
2 tsp. mustard
1 c. low-fat Italian dressing

Mix dressing and pour over salad.

Sweet & Creamy Salad

2 bags romaine lettuce
1 box strawberries, sliced
1 can mandarin oranges, drained
Sugared almonds

 Dressing:
¾ c. mayonnaise
½ c. sugar
⅓ c. red wine vinegar
⅛ c. non-dairy milk
1 T. poppy seeds
1 T. raspberry jam

Mix dressing and pour over lettuce, strawberries and mandarin oranges. Top with sugared almonds.

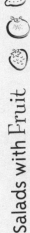

Pasta
Salads

Angel Hair Pasta Salad 1

½ box angel hair pasta, cooked & drained
2 bags European mix
Handful craisins
1 red pepper, diced
Grape tomatoes, cut in half
Baby carrots, sliced

Dressing:
½ c. mayonnaise
¼ c. red wine vinegar
¼ c. sugar
¼ c. water
1 packet Good Seasons roasted garlic

Mix dressing well and pour over salad.

Angel Hair Pasta Salad 2

1 box angel hair pasta
1 bag shredded red cabbage
3 scallions, chopped

Dressing:
¼ c. sugar
¼ c. red wine vinegar
⅓ c. oil
Salt & black pepper to taste

Cook and drain pasta. Mix all ingredients together with pasta.

Spicy Angel Hair Salad

1 box angel hair pasta, cooked & drained
6 garlic cloves, chopped

Dressing:
6 T. soy sauce
6 T. sugar
6 T. vinegar
6 T. oil
½ tsp. crushed red pepper flakes
¼ c. toasted sesame seeds
1 bunch scallions, sliced

Bring dressing to a boil. Pour over chopped garlic cloves and chill. Combine pasta and dressing when ready to serve.

Basil Linguini

1 box linguini
2 tomatoes, chopped
¼ c. olive oil
½ onion, chopped
4 garlic cloves, chopped
5 basil leaves, chopped
1 tsp. salt
Black pepper to taste

Sauté onion and garlic in oil. When onion is translucent, add tomatoes and continue to sauté. Cook pasta and drain. Add vegetables to pasta and mix in basil, salt and black pepper.

Bow Tie Salad

1 box bow tie pasta
Salt & black pepper
1 T. vinegar
1 scallion, diced
1 carrot, grated
2 stalks celery, thinly sliced
2 sour pickles, diced

 Dressing:
1 T. sugar
¼ c. pickle juice
1 c. mayonnaise

Cook pasta with salt, black pepper and 1 Tablespoon vinegar.
Drain and rinse with water. Add vegetables to noodles.
Combine with dressing and chill.

Broccoli with Pasta

1 box linguini
1 T. olive oil
4 - 6 garlic cloves, thinly sliced
1 c. chopped broccoli
Chopped parsley
Salt & black pepper to taste

Cook pasta and drain. Sauté garlic in oil. Add broccoli and
pasta and sauté for a few minutes. Season with parsley, salt and
black pepper.

Japanese Linguini

1 box thin spaghetti
2 yellow peppers
1 red pepper
1 orange pepper
1 green pepper
1 purple pepper
1 c. sesame seeds
4 oz. teriyaki sauce
¼ c. oil

Cook pasta and drain. Slice peppers in strips and grill until black lines appear. Toast sesame seeds in oven until brown. Place all ingredients in bowl, combine Teryiaki sauce and oil, and pour over salad. Mix well.

Macaroni Salad

2 c. macaroni
½ c. mayonnaise
1 T. lemon juice
1 tsp. salt
1 tsp. sugar
1 c. sliced red pepper
½ c. sliced olives
1 tomato, diced

Cook macaroni, drain and rinse with cold water. In a small bowl, mix mayonnaise with lemon juice, salt and sugar. Combine with macaroni, pepper, olives and tomato.

Oriental Salad

1 box spaghetti, cooked & drained
1 package frozen stir fry vegetables, thawed

Sauce:
½ c. light soy sauce
½ tsp. ginger
¼ c. sugar
¼ c. oil

Mix sauce in blender. Pour over pasta and vegetables. Marinate for 2 hours before serving.

Pasta Salad

1 box pasta, any style
4 scallions, sliced
1 red pepper, diced
1 yellow pepper, diced
1 carrot, grated
Handful baby corn
Handful fresh broccoli, chopped
²/₃ c. oil
½ c. vinegar
2 tsp. salt
½ c. sugar
1 tsp. black pepper

Cook pasta and drain. Mix with rest of ingredients.

Pasta & Tuna Salad

1 box spiral pasta, cooked & drained
2 -3 cans tuna, flaked
1 carrot, grated
1 stalk of celery, sliced
2 - 4 scallions, chopped
1 can corn niblets, drained
1 sour pickle, diced
1 red pepper, chopped

 Dressing:
Mayonnaise as desired
Salt & black pepper

Mix all ingredients well.

Pasta with Vegetables

1 box pasta shells
1 avocado, diced
1 box grape tomatoes, halved
1 bunch scallions, sliced
¼ c. olive oil
¾ tsp. salt
¼ tsp. black pepper
½ tsp. onion powder
½ tsp. garlic powder

Cook pasta and drain. Combine with rest of ingredients.

Penne with Tomatoes

1 box penne pasta
1 box grape tomatoes, halved
1 bunch scallions, sliced
2 garlic cloves, crushed
1 T. basil
¼ c. olive oil
Salt & black pepper to taste

Cook pasta and drain. Sauté tomatoes, scallions and garlic.
Add basil, oil, salt and black pepper. Toss over pasta. Serve at
room temperature.

Sesame Noodle Salad

16 oz. angel hair pasta
½ c. sesame oil
¾ c. olive oil
1 T. salt
1 c. chopped fresh cilantro
½ c. chopped scallions
1 c. thinly sliced fresh carrots

Cook pasta and drain. Add sesame oil, olive oil and salt to pasta. Combine cilantro, scallions and carrots, and add to pasta. Chill before serving.

Spicy Penne with Tomatoes

1 box penne pasta
½ box cherry tomatoes, halved
⅓ c. oil
½ tsp. crushed red pepper flakes
2 tsp. salt
1 T. basil
1 T. chopped garlic
½ tsp. black pepper

Cook and drain pasta, and mix with tomatoes. Mix spices into oil and pour over pasta.

Salmon Pasta Salad

1 box angel hair pasta
2 slices salmon
2 c. vegetable broth
1 red pepper, diced
2 T. chopped parsley
3 T. chopped fresh dill
⅓ c. lemon vinaigrette

Vinaigrette:
2 tsp. Dijon mustard
⅔ c. lemon juice
2 tsp. chopped chives
1 tsp. salt
½ tsp. black pepper

Cook pasta. Drain and cool. Broil salmon in lemon vinaigrette, then cool and dice salmon. Combine pasta with vegetables. Mix with vinaigrette, add salmon and toss.

Dairy
Salads

Caesar Salad 1

1 **bag romaine lettuce**
½ **c. grated parmesan cheese**
Croutons

Dressing:
1 **large egg**
1 **garlic clove, crushed**
1 **tsp. Dijon mustard**
⅔ **c. olive oil**
¼ **tsp. vinegar**
Salt & black pepper

Place lettuce, together with half of the Parmesan cheese, in a large bowl. Put egg, garlic and mustard into food processor. Add oil and blend. Add vinegar, salt and black pepper and blend. Pour dressing over salad, and sprinkle rest of cheese on top. Top with croutons.

Caesar Salad 2

1 **bag romaine lettuce**
1 **T. lemon juice**
1 **garlic clove, minced**
½ **tsp. Dijon mustard**
¼ **c. olive oil**
Salt & black pepper to taste
Parmesan cheese

Whisk together lemon juice, garlic and mustard. Slowly add the oil. Mix with lettuce. Add salt and pepper. Crumble cheese on top.

Carrot Salad

1 ½ lbs. carrots, peeled & cut into chunks
1 ½ lbs. parsnips, peeled & cut into chunks
2 T. olive oil
2 T. ground cumin
2 T. kosher salt
1 tsp. black pepper
¼ c. chopped fresh cilantro
3 garlic cloves, minced
½ c. crumbled feta cheese

Preheat oven to 400 degrees. Place all ingredients except cheese in bowl and mix well. Spread mixture onto large ungreased pan. Bake for 45 minutes. Add feta cheese when done. Serve hot.

Creamy Dressing

1 c. mayonnaise
2 T. sugar
2 T. vinegar
¼ tsp. salt
1 T. milk
1 tsp. paprika
½ tsp. mustard

Blend all ingredients. Refrigerate until ready to serve.

Dairy Dressing

2 T. lemon juice
1 garlic clove, crushed
⅔ c. lowfat natural yogurt
2 T. olive oil
Salt & black pepper to taste

Combine all ingredients.

Dairy Salads

Feta Cheese Salad

2 bags euro mix
1 box grape tomatoes
1 avocado, diced
6 - 8 scallions, cut into small rings
3 oz. crumbled feta cheese

 Dressing:
3 T. red wine vinegar
¼ c. olive oil
1 garlic clove, crushed
1 tsp. Dijon mustard
1 T. mayonnaise
Salt & black pepper to taste

Place vegetables in bowl. Mix dressing and pour over salad. Crumble feta cheese on top.

Greek Salad 1

1 purple onion, sliced
1 red pepper, cut into chunks
1 green pepper, cut into chunks
1 box cherry tomatoes
2 cucumbers, sliced
½ c. crumbled feta cheese
1 garlic clove, minced
½ c. black olives

Dressing:
¼ c. red wine vinegar
2 T. chopped fresh dill
1 tsp. oregano
⅓ c. olive oil
Salt & black pepper to taste

In large bowl, place vegetables, cheese, garlic and olives. Pour dressing over salad and toss well.

Greek Salad 2

1 bag romaine lettuce
1 medium purple onion
1 cucumber, sliced
1 tomato, sliced
3 T. sliced black olives
1 container feta cheese

Dressing:
½ c. olive oil
3 T. lemon juice
1 T. garlic powder
1 T. onion powder
½ tsp. black pepper
1 tsp. salt

Place lettuce in bowl. Chop onions, then add cucumbers, tomatoes and olives. Crumble cheese on top. Pour dressing over salad just before serving.

Greek Salad 3

4 tomatoes, sliced
1 cucumber, peeled & sliced
1 small purple onion, sliced
Black olives
Feta cheese, cubed

Dressing:
3 T. olive oil
1 T. lemon juice
½ tsp. oregano
Salt & black pepper

Mix dressing and pour over salad. Place feta cheese on top.

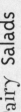

Orange Salad

1 bag spinach leaves
½ c. sliced ripe olives
½ c. sliced purple onions
1 can mandarin oranges, drained
½ c. balsamic vinegar
Dash black pepper
¼ c. feta cheese

Mix ingredients together. Crumble feta cheese on top.

Potato Salad

3 lbs. small red potatoes

 Dressing:
½ c. sour cream
½ c. mayonnaise
Chopped fresh dill
4 scallions, thinly sliced
2 tsp. salt
Black pepper to taste

Boil potatoes and drain. Place in bowl. Mix dressing very well and pour over potatoes.

Poppy Seed Salad

1 bag salad greens
1 purple onion, sliced
1 c. craisins

 Dressing:
½ c. mayonnaise
⅓ c. sugar
¼ c. milk
2 T. vinegar
1 T. poppy seeds

Blend dressing ingredients and pour over salad.

Sour Cream Dip

¾ c. sour cream
¾ c. diced cucumbers
1 tsp. dill
⅛ tsp. black pepper
1 T. parsley
1 tsp. lemon juice
¼ c. sugar

Blend all ingredients together.

Salads with Meats

Salads with Meats

Caesar Chicken Salad

1 **package chicken cutlets**
2 **T. mayonnaise**
2 **T. mustard**
1 **bag romaine lettuce**
Salt & paprika
Cornflake crumbs
Olive oil

Cut chicken cutlets into strips and sprinkle with salt and paprika. Mix mayonnaise and mustard. Dip cutlets into mayonnaise and mustard mixture. Coat with cornflake crumbs. Grease 9" x 13" baking pan. Place cutlets in pan in single layer. Sprinkle with olive oil. Bake 10 minutes on each side. Cut into bite-sized pieces.

 Dressing:
1 **garlic clove, crushed**
3 **T. lemon juice**
2 **T. olive oil**
1/3 **c. chicken broth**
2 **tsp. mustard**
1 **tsp. steak sauce**
1/2 **tsp. black pepper**

Place romaine lettuce into bowl. Mix dressing and pour over lettuce. Place warm chicken on top.

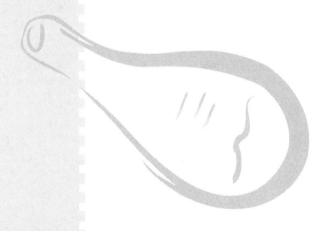

Chef Salad

1 bag romaine lettuce
1 box grape tomatoes
shredded cold cuts, as desired
croutons

Dressing:
⅛ c. red wine vinegar
⅛ c. honey
⅛ c. sugar
½ c. oil
½ c. Dijon mustard
Salt & black pepper to taste

Combine vegetables with cold cuts. Mix dressing and pour over
the salad. Place croutons on top.

Creamy Chef Salad

1 bag romaine lettuce
1 container of cherry tomatoes
1 purple onion, sliced
¼ lb. turkey breast, sliced
¼ lb. pastrami, sliced
Onion garlic croutons

Dressing:
1 tsp. mayonnaise
1 T. chopped scallions
½ tsp. dry mustard
1 tsp. sugar
1 T. chopped parsley
¼ c. oil
2 garlic cloves, crushed
1 tsp. lemon juice

Combine vegetables with meat. Mix dressing and pour over
salad. Mix well. Place croutons on top.

Chicken Salad 1

Chicken cutlets
1 bottle Italian dressing
1 bag lettuce
1 can baby corn, drained
1 box cherry tomatoes
Chinese noodles

 Dressing:
¼ c. sugar
less than ¼ c. oil
¼ c. vinegar
2 squirts of mustard
1 garlic clove, chopped

Mix chicken cutlets with Italian dressing. Broil and cut into strips. Add to vegetables. Mix dressing well and pour over salad. Sprinkle Chinese noodles on top.

Chicken Salad 2

3 chicken cutlets
1 bag romaine lettuce

Sauce:
2 T. lemon juice
2 T. honey
¼ tsp. curry powder
Salt & black pepper to taste

Pour sauce over chicken and marinate for 1 hour. Grill chicken, slice and place over lettuce.

Chicken Romaine Salad

3 c. cubed cooked chicken breast
⅓ c. chopped red pepper
¼ c. chopped celery
¼ c. chopped scallions
1 bag romaine lettuce

Dressing:
¾ c. mayonnaise
2 tsp. grated horseradish
1 ½ tsp. lemon juice
1 garlic clove, crushed
½ tsp. salt
¼ tsp. black pepper

In large bowl, combine chicken, pepper, celery and scallions.
Combine dressing ingredients in blender. Mix chicken mixture
with lettuce. Add dressing just before serving.

Chinese Chicken Salad I

1 package chicken cutlets, cubed
Soy sauce

Salad:
1 bag lettuce
1 bag romaine lettuce
1 can baby corn, drained
4 cucumbers, sliced
2 tomatoes, sliced

Dressing:
¼ c. sugar
¼ c. oil
¼ c. vinegar
⅛ c. soy sauce
Drop of garlic powder

Dip chicken in soy sauce and broil 7 - 10 minutes on each side.
Place salad in bowl. Add cubed chicken. Pour dressing over
salad just before serving.

Chinese Chicken Salad 2

1 lb. chicken cutlets
Soy sauce
1 bag lettuce
Sugar snap peas
1 red pepper
½ can baby corn
1 cucumber

 Dressing:
¼ c. sugar
¼ c. oil
⅛ c. soy sauce
4 garlic cloves, crushed

Broil chicken cutlets in soy sauce. Mix chicken with vegetables.
Pour dressing over chicken mixture.

Cold Cut Salad

1 lb. assorted cold cuts
1 bag romaine lettuce
1 c. croutons

Dressing:
¾ c. oil
¼ c. honey
¼ c. sugar
¼ c. red wine vinegar
½ tsp. salt
1 T. Dijon mustard

Mix dressing and pour over salad. Top with croutons.

Deli Salad

1 bag romaine lettuce
Various colored peppers, cut into strips
1 box cherry tomatoes
Sugar snap peas
1 purple onion, sliced
1 lb. turkey and pastrami

Dressing:
1 T. Dijon mustard
½ tsp. salt
¾ c. oil
¼ c. honey
¼ c. sugar
⅛ c. red wine vinegar

Mix vegetables and meat in bowl. Mix dressing and pour over salad.

Euro Deli Salad I

1 package romaine lettuce
½ box grape tomatoes
4 - 5 slices pastrami, shredded
4 - 5 slices turkey breast, shredded

Dressing:
¼ c. honey
¼ c. sugar
¼ c. wine vinegar
1 T. mustard
½ tsp. salt
¾ c. olive oil

Blend dressing and pour over salad. Place meat on top.

Euro Deli Salad 2

1 bag romaine lettuce
¼ lb. deli meat of choice

Dressing:
¼ c. mustard
¼ c. oil
½ tsp. white wine
½ tsp. brown sugar
¼ c. sugar
¼ c. honey
¼ c. red wine vinegar

Mix dressing well and pour over lettuce. Cut meat and place on top of salad. Chill until ready to serve.

Spicy Deli Salad

1 head romaine lettuce
½ box grape tomatoes
1 yellow pepper, cubed
¼ lb. turkey breast, sliced
¼ lb. pastrami, sliced
1 c. onion garlic croutons

Dressing:
2 T. mayonnaise
¼ c. oil
½ tsp. dry mustard
2-3 tsp. teriyaki sauce
2 garlic cloves, crushed
1 T. lemon juice

Mix vegetables and meat in bowl. Mix dressing and pour over salad. Top with croutons.

Grilled Chicken
& Spinach Salad

3 oz. chicken breast
2 c. spinach leaves
1 tsp. toasted pine nuts
1 T. olive oil
Salt & black pepper to taste
½ lemon

Grill chicken and place over spinach leaves. Mix nuts, olive oil, salt and black pepper and sprinkle on top of salad. Squeeze the lemon on top.

Herbed Grilled Chicken Salad

1 package chicken cutlets, cut into strips

Marinade:
3 T. olive oil
2 garlic cloves, minced
2 T. apple cider vinegar
¼ c. mustard
2 T. chopped chives
2 T. dried rosemary
⅓ c. honey

Mix marinade ingredients. Add to chicken. Grill marinated chicken 7 – 10 minutes on each side.

1 bag lettuce
Pine nuts
1 can mandarin oranges, drained
½ c. diced purple onion

Dressing:
4 T. red wine vinegar
4 T. brown sugar
¼ c. olive oil

Mix salad ingredients. Mix dressing ingredients. Add chicken strips to salad. Pour dressing over salad.

Oriental Grilled Chicken Salad

1 package chicken cutlets
Soy sauce

Marinate chicken in soy sauce for 1 hour. Broil chicken for 5 minutes on each side. Cool and dice.

Salad:
1 bag romaine lettuce
1 red pepper, cut into strips
1 can baby corn, drained & cut in half
1 cucumber, sliced
1 can bamboo shoots, drained
½ package snow peas

 Dressing:
Dash garlic powder
¼ c. sugar
¼ c. oil
¼ c. vinegar
⅛ c. soy sauce

Combine vegetables and chicken in bowl. Mix dressing and pour over salad just before serving.

Turkey Caesar Salad

1 bag romaine lettuce
Shredded smoked turkey
Croutons

 Dressing:
¼ c. mayonnaise
2 T. Dijon mustard
¼ c. oil
1 tsp. salt
¼ tsp. crushed garlic
black pepper
Sprinkle of Mrs. Dash

Combine lettuce and meat in bowl. Mix dressing and pour over salad. Add croutons on top.

Dips & Dressings

Avocado Dip

2 avocados
½ small onion, finely diced
1 tomato, finely diced
Juice of 1 lemon
Salt, black pepper & garlic powder to taste

Mash avocado and add diced vegetables. Season with lemon juice and spices.

Avocado Guacamole Dip

2 avocados, mashed
¼ c. finely chopped onions
2 small jalapeño peppers, seeded and minced
2 small tomatoes, finely chopped
3 T. lemon juice
1 garlic clove, minced
2 T. chopped cilantro
Salt to taste

Combine all ingredients.

Balsamic Vinaigrette Dressing

½ c. + 2 T. olive oil
⅓ c. balsamic vinegar
1 T. minced shallot
1 tsp. minced fresh marjoram

Mix ingredients well. (This dressing goes well with portobello mushrooms and lettuce.)

Caesar Dressing

1 T. mayonnaise
1 T. mustard
¼ c. oil
¼ c. water
Salt, sugar, garlic powder & oregano to taste

Mix ingredients well and use with any salad greens.

Creamy Dip

½ c. mayonnaise
1 T. chopped sour pickle
1 T. chopped onion
1 T. chopped parsley

Mix ingredients together.

Diet Creamy Dressing

1 c. mayonnaise
¼ c. vinegar
¼ c. water
1 heaping T. garlic powder
½ T. Splenda
Dash salt

Mix ingredients well.

Dill Dip

¾ c. mayonnaise
1 bunch scallions, chopped
½ c. chopped fresh dill
1 T. lemon juice

Blend all ingredients. Refrigerate.

Easy Dill Dressing

1 c. mayonnaise
1 T. dill
1 T. sugar
3 T. red wine vinegar
2 - 3 garlic cloves, crushed
1 tsp. salt
½ tsp. black pepper

Blend all ingredients.

Easy Lemon Garlic Dressing

1 c. olive oil
⅓ c. red wine vinegar
1 garlic clove, crushed
Dash dill, lemon juice & oregano
1 tsp. salt
1 tsp. black pepper

Mix ingredients together.

Easy Mustard Dressing

1 garlic clove, crushed
2 T. vinegar
1 tsp. mustard
6 T. oil
Salt & black pepper

Mix first three ingredients until smooth. Add oil, salt and black pepper and mix well.

Easy Tart Dressing

2 garlic cloves, chopped
½ c. oil
1 T. sugar
½ tsp. soy sauce
¼ tsp. vinegar
1 tsp. salt
1 tsp. black pepper
1 tsp. mustard

Blend all ingredients in blender.

Eggplant Dip

2 eggplants
1 tsp. salt
Juice of ½ lemon
1 T. mayonnaise
4 garlic cloves, minced

Broil eggplant for 1 hour, turning every 10 minutes. Cool.
Scoop out flesh and mash with rest of ingredients.

Eggplant Relish

2 eggplants, peeled & cubed
2 zucchinis, peeled & cubed
1 large onion, diced
1 green pepper, diced
Oil
½ c. ketchup
1 T. sugar
1 c. hot water
Salt & black pepper to taste

Sauté vegetables in oil. Add rest of ingredients
and simmer for a few minutes.

Garlic Dressing

⅓ c. vinegar
½ c. olive oil
1 tsp. lemon juice
½ tsp. cumin
2 garlic cloves, crushed
Salt & black pepper to taste
Garlic powder & oregano to taste

Combine all ingredients in jar. Shake well.

Green Pickle Dip

1 c. mayonnaise
1 onion, chopped
Handful fresh dill, chopped
2 sour pickles, diced

Mix ingredients well.

Green Pickle & Olive Dip

1 T. chopped sour pickle
1 T. chopped onion
1 T. chopped parsley
1 T. chopped stuffed green olives
½ c. mayonnaise

Mix ingredients well and chill.

Honey Mustard Dressing

¾ c. mayonnaise
3 T. honey
3 T. mustard
1 T. lemon juice
Salt & black pepper to taste

Mix ingredients well.

Lemon Dressing

²/₃ c. olive oil
2 tsp. sugar
1 tsp. salt
1 tsp. mustard
¼ tsp. black pepper
¼ c. lemon juice

Mix ingredients together.

Maple Raspberry Dressing

4 T. raspberry vinegar
4 T. maple syrup
4 T. olive oil
4 T. oil
2 tsp. Dijon mustard
½ tsp. salt

Mix ingredients together.

Parsley Dip

1 c. mayonnaise
1 T. mustard
¼ tsp. crushed fresh garlic
1 T. lemon juice
½ tsp. sugar
1 bunch parsley
Salt to taste

Blend ingredients in blender.

Parsley Dressing

3 T. olive oil
2 T. lemon juice
¼ tsp. onion powder
2 T. chopped parsley

Blend all ingredients.

Russian Dressing

1 c. mayonnaise
½ c. ketchup
1 tsp. garlic powder

Mix ingredients well.

Salad Dressing

¼ c. balsamic vinegar
¼ c. olive oil
¼ c. water
¼ c. sugar
½ tsp. dry mustard
½ tsp. garlic powder
Dash salt & black pepper

Mix ingredients well.

Scallion Dip

2 c. mayonnaise
4 T. chopped scallions, including green parts
6 T. chopped fresh parsley
3 garlic cloves

Blend 1 cup mayonnaise with scallions and parsley. Add second cup together with garlic cloves and blend well.

Spinach Artichoke Dip

1 bag chopped spinach
2 cans artichoke hearts, drained

 Dressing:
¾ c. mayonnaise
1 T. lemon juice
4 garlic cloves, crushed
Salt & black pepper to taste

Cook spinach in water until water boils. Drain spinach. Chop off ½ inch of leaves from artichokes and discard. Chop artichokes. Mix artichokes and spinach. Mix dressing with vegetables.

Crunchy Spinach Dip

2 c. mayonnaise
½ c. chopped onions
½ c. chopped green pepper
½ c. chopped parsley
1 box spinach, thawed

Combine ingredients and blend well.

Easy Spinach Dip

1 box chopped frozen spinach, thawed & drained
½ c. finely chopped onion
Finely chopped parsley to taste
2 c. mayonnaise

Mix spinach, onion and parsley. Add mayonnaise and marinate overnight.

Spinach Onion Dip

2 c. mayonnaise
¼ c. parsley flakes
½ package onion soup mix
1 garlic clove, diced
½ T. lemon juice
10 oz. chopped spinach, thawed and drained
black pepper to taste

Blend ingredients well.

Spinach Parsley Dip

10 oz. frozen chopped spinach
1 small onion, grated
1 garlic clove
1 ½ T. lemon juice
⅓ tsp. black pepper
2 c. mayonnaise
½ c. fresh parsley

Thaw spinach and squeeze out excess water. Blend all ingredients together.

Dips & Dressings

Sun-Dried Tomato & Basil Spread

1 c. oil-packed sun-dried tomatoes, drained
1 c. fresh basil leaves
¼ c. pine nuts, toasted
1 ½ T. olive oil
1 T. balsamic vinegar
2 large garlic cloves
1 tsp. lemon juice
Saly & black pepper

Chop first seven ingredients in food processor until they form a coarse paste. Season with salt and black pepper.

Crunchy Tomato Dip

1 large onion, diced
1 celery, diced
1 large tomato, diced
2 garlic cloves, minced
Olive oil

Sauté vegetables in olive oil.

Add:
1 squirt ketchup
½ c. water
½ tsp. salt
4 shakes salad seasonings

Crushed Tomato & Pepper Dip

1 can crushed tomatoes
4 green peppers, chopped
½ c. oil
2 T. crushed garlic
Drop of salt
1 T. paprika
1 tsp. cumin
Dash hot red pepper

Cook ingredients on top of stove for 20 minutes until thick. Cool.

Hot Tomato Dip

4 tomatoes
1 jalapeño pepper
2 garlic cloves
1 T. olive oil
¼ tsp. vinegar
Salt to taste

Blend tomatoes in food processor. Pour most of tomatoes into bowl, leaving some in food processor. Add jalapeño pepper and garlic cloves to tomatoes in food processor and blend well. Pour this mixture into bowl containing rest of tomatoes. Add rest of ingredients and mix well.

Vinaigrette Dressing

1 T. wine vinegar
3 T. olive oil
Salt & black pepper to taste

Dissolve salt in vinegar. Slowly blend in oil and season with black pepper.

Dips & Dressings

Index of
Recipes

Index of Recipes

Index of Recipes

Index of Recipes

Notes/Personal Recipes

Notes/Personal Recipes

Notes/Personal Recipes

Notes/Personal Recipes